OLIVIA IN FIVE SEVEN FIVE: AUTISM IN HAIKU

A haiku chapbook

poems by

Kathie Giorgio

Finishing Line Press
Georgetown, Kentucky

OLIVIA IN FIVE SEVEN FIVE: AUTISM IN HAIKU

A haiku chapbook

Copyright © 2022 by Kathie Giorgio
ISBN 978-1-64662-852-0 First Edition
All rights reserved under International and Pan-American Copyright Conventions. No part of this book may be reproduced in any manner whatsoever without written permission from the publisher, except in the case of brief quotations embodied in critical articles and reviews.

Publisher: Leah Huete de Maines

Editor: Christen Kincaid

Cover Art: Photograph by Michael Giorgio

Author Photo: Ron Wimmer, Wimmer Photography

Cover Design: Elizabeth Maines McCleavy

Order online: www.finishinglinepress.com
also available on amazon.com

Author inquiries and mail orders:
Finishing Line Press
PO Box 1626
Georgetown, Kentucky 40324
USA

Table of Contents

Introduction	1
Olivia Defines Autism	2
Autism out Loud	3
So Much More	4
Vive Le Difference	5
From The Beginning	6
Perfectly Fine	7
Glorious Blue	8
Sing It!	9
Rebel	10
Watching in Awe	11
Stim Stories	12
Only a Name	13
Eyes Opened	14
IEP Hell	15
Soon	16
More than a Cry	17
Communication	18
Path	19
Eruption	20
Expression	21
Not At All	22
Thank You	23
Miracle	24
She Grows	25
Credit Where Credit's Due	26
Blunt	27
Alike	28
Always Proud	29
So Much More	30
Autism Awareness Month	31
Just For Fun	32
A Poem in Olivia's Voice: She Holds the Infinite World	33

FOR OLIVIA, of course
And for all the Olivias in the world
And your parents too

INTRODUCTION

In the pivotal year 2000, I gave birth to my fourth child, Olivia. My other children, from my first marriage, were 16 years old, 14 years old and 13 years old, so it had been a while since I dealt with a newborn. Even so, it was very clear that Olivia was different. Soon after turning a year old, Olivia was diagnosed with autism.

It was devastating for her father and for me. We are both writers, and when we were told that our daughter would be nonverbal, looking at us as if we were "bumps on a log", we were horrified. But we saw things with Olivia; verbalizations that mimicked our speech, taps on our shoes and arms and knees to make sure we were paying attention, facial expressions and outstretched arms. We decided that we would treat Olivia as Olivia. It was just who she was.

Olivia went to an early childhood program at one of our public schools, and then she continued there through the 5th grade. We never put Olivia in any special therapies or put her on medication. We simply paid attention to how she learned and who she was. At school, she was 100% mainstreamed, only leaving for the special ed room at her own volition, when she felt she was overwhelmed or needed help. The school was amazing, eagerly joining in with our different way of looking at how to treat our different girl.

When this book is released, Olivia will be almost 22 years old and a senior in college, majoring in art therapy. She attends college fully on grants and scholarships that she earned through her academic and artistic achievements. She made Dean's List in her first year of college, and has made it every semester since. She is a gifted violinist, guitarist, and ukulele player. She's written a novel, had her poetry published, and her artwork is stupendous. She knows she is autistic and she embraces it, using her differences to bring change to the world.

One year, in April, which is both National Poetry Month and Autism Awareness Month, I challenged myself to writing a haiku a day about Olivia and about autism. *Olivia In Five, Seven, Five* is the result. This little chapbook holds a mother's love and grief, a child's challenges, and triumph.

I hope you like it. So does Olivia.

OLIVIA DEFINES AUTISM

"My brain slips sideways,"
she said when she was seven.
Autism explained.

AUTISM OUT LOUD

"She might be silent,"
they told us. Our hearts broke. But
she smiled brave. And sang!

SO MUCH MORE

There is so much more
than autism in her eyes.
Olivia glows!

VIVE LA DIFFERENCE

Awareness? Please, more.
Accept. Appreciate. And
embrace difference.

FROM THE BEGINNING

"Dumbass." Her first word.
Not "Mama." Should have known then
this ride would be wild.

PERFECTLY FINE

My daughter is not an epidemic. She is autistic. Not sick.

GLORIOUS BLUE

Autism's color
is blue. But she doesn't make
me sad. She's my joy.

SING IT!

My daughter's first song?
The theme from Cops. Autism
is bad-ass, baby.

REBEL

Rules of the Haiku:
Syllables five seven five.
But autism has no rules, so I can write about my girl forever
and ever amen. HA!

WATCHING IN AWE

Her shirt says, "I can."
It says, "And I will." On back,
"Watch me." Oh, I do.

STIM STORIES

Baby told stories
on her back. Hands, feet, stimming.
Now she writes books. Still.

ONLY A NAME

The World sticks labels.
Autism. Asperger's. But
my girl is not stuck.

EYES OPENED

I had three babies.
Thought I knew it all. But then
Four showed me the Truth.

IEP HELL

IEPs. "Your child
can't do this. Doesn't do that."
See what she does, please.

SOON

Sad little girl face.
Her world and ours still apart.
Collision - joy - soon.

MORE THAN A CRY

Baby's cry. Chaos
voice in new world's wilderness.
Autistic unrest.

COMMUNICATION

Stimming. Hand-ballet.
Autistic sign language. Watch!
Flutters speak volumes.

PATH

She stood up rows of
toy bears. Colored puzzle paths.
Her mind wove with them.

ERUPTION

Meltdown. On the floor.
Autism takeover. Words
won't touch what she feels.

EXPRESSION

She paints Starry Night
in pink. Teacher shakes her head.
We say, "Beautiful!"

NOT AT ALL

The first time she called
herself disabled, we cried.
Abled! No dis here.

THANK YOU

Never thought I'd be
autism articulate.
First, scared. Now, grateful.

MIRACLE

I look at my girl.
I don't see Autism. I
see a Miracle.

SHE GROWS

We walk in Springtime.
See fish leap. Ducks mate. Buds. Her
blush is the future.

CREDIT WHERE CREDIT'S DUE

Doc says, "Write a book
on how you beat Autism."
We didn't. She did.

BLUNT

Autism stands out.
No filter on its feelings.
Autism is Truth.

ALIKE

We're all different.
Autism is different.
What's the difference?

ALWAYS PROUD

When she was born, we felt pride and joy. Autism hasn't changed our minds.

SO MUCH MORE

She's Hyperbole.
Autism exaggerates.
Means there's more to love.

AUTISM AWARENESS MONTH

April. One month. But
Autism is day by day.
Forever April.

JUST FOR FUN

Autism. Aw-tiz-
Um. Autism. Autism.
Autism. Haiku.

A POEM IN OLIVIA'S VOICE
SHE HOLDS THE INFINITE WORLD

By Olivia Giorgio

She was told that she wouldn't make it to college
That she wouldn't look at other people normally
That she would see others as rocks, emotionless and still

Her parents were disappointed in the response
But continued to hold onto hope and belief in their daughter
Because they could see the infinite worlds she holds

Years later when her parents told her she was autistic
She couldn't believe the negative things she read and heard
But the depressing words she heard and read didn't let her down

She continued to rise and prove others wrong over and over
Through her art and intellect
She proved herself to be more than just capable of living a normal life

Her parents continue to support her through adulthood
And remind her of how proud they are of her
That her autism won't hold her back
But push her forward

She remembers those messages her parents told her
In her infinite world
And hopes that those messages can reach others like her

KATHIE GIORGIO is the critically acclaimed author of six novels, *The Home For Wayward Clocks* (The Main Street Rag Publishing Company 2011), *Learning To Tell (A Life)Time* (The Main Street Rag Publishing Company 2013), *Rise From The River* (The Main Street Rag Publishing Company 2015), *In Grace's Time* (Black Rose Writing 2017), *If You Tame Me* (Black Rose Writing 2019), and *All Told* (Austin Macauley 2021), two story collections, *Enlarged Hearts* (The Main Street Rag Publishing Company 2012) and *Oddities & Endings; The Collected Stories Of Kathie Giorgio* (The Main Street Rag Publishing Company 2016), a collection of essays, *Today's Moment Of Happiness Despite The News; A Year Of Spontaneous Essays* (Black Rose Writing 2018), and three poetry books, *True Light Falls In Many Forms* (The Main Street Rag Publishing Company 2016), *When You Finally Said No* (Finishing Line Press 2019), and *No Matter Which Way You Look, There Is More To See* (Finishing Line Press 2020). In March of 2023, Giorgio's seventh novel, *Hope Always Rises*, will be released by Moonshine Cove Press. Giorgio's short stories and poems have appeared in countless literary magazines and anthologies. Her short story, *Snapdragon*, was performed on stage for the *Stories On Stage* series at Su Teatro theatre in Boulder, Colorado. Her poem, "Harvest Moon," was included in the Poetry Leaves exhibition in Waterford, Michigan, in 2020. She's been nominated in both fiction and poetry for the Pushcart Prize, the Write Well Award, the Million Writer Award, and for both fiction and poetry for the *Best of the Net Anthology*. Her novel *The Home For Wayward Clocks* won the 2011 Outstanding Achievement Award from the Wisconsin Library Association. Her novel *In Grace's Time* was runner-up in fiction in the 2017 Maxy Award and the second place winner of the 2017 Silver Pen Award For Literary Excellence. Her novel *If You Tame Me* won second place in the Women's Fiction category of the Pencraft Awards For Literary Excellence. Her poem, "Light," was runner-up in *Rosebud Magazine's* 2021 Poetry competition, and her poem, Again, won first prize in the Wisconsin Writers Association's Jade Ring contest. Her short story, *Recipe*, won Honorable Mention in the 2021 Zona Gale Short Story Award for the Council for Wisconsin Writers.

Recently, Giorgio was listed as one of the top 21 Wisconsin writers of the 21st century by the Milwaukee Journal Sentinel.

She lives in Waukesha, Wisconsin, with her husband, mystery writer Michael Giorgio, their daughter Olivia, who is writing her first novel, a neurotic dog named after Ursula Le Guin, a fat cat named Edgar Allen Paw, and a tiny cat named Muse.

Besides writer, Giorgio is also the director and founder of the international creative writing studio, AllWriters' Workplace & Workshop LLC. AllWriters' offers online and on-site courses and workshops in all genres and abilities of creative writing, as well as coaching and editing services. Thousands of writers worldwide have gotten their start at AllWriters', and thousands have continued their career there. Giorgio has taught for 27 years. She also paints, primarily in acrylics, though she has a fondness for painting mannequins.

www.ingramcontent.com/pod-product-compliance
Ingram Content Group UK Ltd.
Pitfield, Milton Keynes, MK11 3LW, UK
UKHW041303180426
11947UKWH00009B/646